PRAYER WITHOUT PRETENDING

By the same author:

ONCE BITTEN

PRAYER WITHOUT PRETENDING

by Anne J. Townsend

SCRIPTURE UNION

47 Marylebone Lane, London W1M 6AX

© Anne J. Townsend 1973

First published 1973

Reprinted 1973

Reprinted 1974

ISBN 0 85421 293 0

Printed by A. McLay & Co., Ltd., Cardiff and London

CONTENTS

AUTHOR'S NOTE

SOMEONE reading this may well ask the question, 'How did the Overseas Missionary Fellowship ever come to accept such a person as one of their missionaries'?

I often ask myself this question too!

I am not the type of person worthy of the privilege of being a successor in the long line of spiritual giants, stretching back over the hundred years since Hudson Taylor first founded the China Inland Mission (now O.M.F.). The realization of this is sometimes awesome to someone like me.

I constantly marvel that *God* calls, and uses, people like me. He takes us as we are and shapes our lives, making us slowly more like Himself. He called me to Thailand; and waited until I was already a missionary to challenge, and make me consider, intercessory prayer.

So, please don't hold the O.M.F. Candidates' Committee responsible for my ignorance! When I came before them, I could say in all honesty that I unquestioningly accepted all that I had been told that the Bible taught. I had no questions then as to the value of intercession. *Since then*, God has led me to think through many issues for myself, instead of blindly accepting what I had been told. This has sometimes involved me in periods of doubt; but I have emerged stronger for this. I now know very clearly that I must pray for others, and why I must.

The lesson might have been learnt long ago . . . but my Teacher has only reached this point with me in the last few years.

A slow learner? Probably! And still learning!

My deep gratitude goes to my husband, John, without whose encouragement this book would never have been written; to Yvonne Gaudraux, without whom this book would never have been typed; and to many friends whose stories and thoughts are part of this book.

Anne Townsend
O.M.F. Christian Hospital, Manorom, Thailand. 1972

1. FAILURE

SHE was dead.

I was powerless to bring her back to life. Was her death a terrible waste; or might it ever bear fruit? I had never been overwhelmed before by such a depth of guilt at my thoughtless neglect.

My shame would have diminished had I not just been criticizing other people for failing in the very thing I had omitted to do myself. I had never prayed seriously for this friend.

The evening before she died, my husband and I had driven home through the pouring rain of an English autumn evening. The sheets of water obscuring our vision reminded us of our previous four years spent working as missionary doctors in Thailand, where rain never drizzles, only drenches.

We chatted aimlessly at first, deriving comfort from the womb-like security of the car. Finally we brought our deepest thoughts out into the open; we had to admit our amazement and depression at the lack of care and concern expressed by the group of Christians we had visited that evening. They had written occasionally, saying that they were praying for us. We accepted their leader's letters at their face value, and were sure that the group prayed for us. The truth hit home in painful blows with every question fired at us by group members. We were forced to ask ourselves, 'Could they have been praying for us when they don't know how many children we have; in what part of Thailand we had been working; nor whether we had gone through the struggle of learning the Thai language?'

We answered their questions readily enough, trying to maintain bland expressions, and masking the flame of dismay kindled by their ignorance. Their interest in us was obviously only superficial. Had we been naïve in counting on them as *real* prayer supporters? They had obviously never prayed with the concerned interest that their leader's letters led us to assume.

We were just home on our first leave from Thailand, and were still vulnerable and sensitive to the heartbreaks that so-called 'missionary deputation work' can bring. Later on, such a group would not have caught us off our guard. We developed a greater resilience; and were able to find good in situations that might have distressed us earlier. That night was our initiation into the shattering of our illusions about some on whom we had been counting for real prayer support. It was our first encounter with a group who supported us on paper, but whose support in reality was barely paper-thin.

We tried to make excuses for them to one another, muttering comments about 'busy people', 'full lives', and 'many other interests'. However, basically, though I did not realize it at the time, I was upset and critical. Why had they *pretended* that they cared, when in reality they did not?

As my husband steered the car up the drive into my parents' garden, I noticed my father waiting for us on the doorstep.

'Someone wants you to 'phone immediately'. He handed me a name on a piece of paper.

'Strange,' I thought, 'That's my friend's *brother's* name. What in the world does he want with me at this time of night?'

I blithely entered my father's study to telephone, emerging later numbed by the conversation. My friend's family had received a telegram that evening from Ethiopia, saying that she was critically ill.

I had known that she had been ill with infective hepatitis because she had written to tell me about it. I had genuinely intended to pray for her recovery as she had requested me to; but my good intentions had been submerged in the flood of work involved in caring for my family of three lively children. The two pre-schoolers seemed up to permanent mischief: being new to England from tropical village life, they had no idea that open fires burnt, that pneumonia might develop from playing in the white crisp icing in the garden called 'snow', if they ran out barefooted and coatless; or that roads were meant for *real* cars, and not for little boys fresh from Thailand to use as motorways for toy ones.

My good intentions had been dissipated in the energy needed to adapt again to life in England after life in Thailand. I could find excuses by the hundred for not having prayed for my friend.

Yet, as I lay sleepless throughout the long night, praying desperately for my friend's recovery, I began to realize that I must face up to reality. The truth was stark; it shattered my self-image of myself, a missionary. Honesty forced me to admit that I had never really prayed much for this friend. I had promised to . . . but somehow, praying for her, or for anyone else, was low down on my list of priorities for any day's activities. Family, medical work, entertaining, language study, and writing, left little time for praying.

I felt even worse because I was assured that this friend *did* pray for me. She was the rare sort of person who said she would do something and could be depended upon to act true to her word. The card that came to Thailand promptly on my birthday annually was clear enough indication that she cared enough not to forget. My love had not enfolded her, as hers had me.

I was humbled to realize that I had just been inwardly criticizing the group we had visited that evening for not caring for me, although my relationship with them had never been close. Yet, at the same time, my love had failed to reach out to one who had been a close friend in student days.

I prayed frantically through the night, sleeping in snatches. When the telephone rang in the morning bringing news of my friend's death, I was too exhausted to react. I felt blank and empty. I had failed to care for her, and somehow I felt partly to blame for her death.

'But why?' I could not stop asking myself, 'Why . . .

Why . . . Why . . .?'

Questions exploded in my mind and would not be quenched, 'Why did she die? Why did *she* die? Where was God when I was praying, why didn't He answer? Anyway, should an omnipotent God want us to pray . . . surely He can get on without my feeble prayers?'

I was forced to admit to myself, that although I was a missionary serving with the Overseas Missionary Fellowship whose roots are grounded in intercession, and whose history is full of spectacular answers to prayer, yet I did not really understand very much about intercessory prayer.

I had given verbal assent to the efficacy and importance of it, because I had grown up in a Christian subculture at University, in which Christian members of this group unquestioningly prayed for other people. I had, on becoming a missionary, sent out the usual circular letters giving requests for prayer; both because it was expected, and because I could see that there were many advantages in this practice. Yet, if I was to admit the truth, I had to face the fact that I knew next to nothing about intercessory prayer; neither in theory nor in practice.

At the time when my friend died, I was trying hard to be honest with myself as a Christian, and to remove those trappings of hypocrisy in Christian living that made me pretend to be what I was not. I therefore decided that if I did not fully believe there was any point in praying for other people, then I should stop it; so I ceased. Yet the subject would not get out of my mind. It endlessly revolved in my thoughts, and repeatedly confronted me, until in desperation for some kind of solution with which to live as a missionary, I was forced to begin to face the problems and to try to think them through for myself. I could not run away from it. However, having thought and thought, I discovered a strange reluctance to share my findings in writing. What Christian *likes* admitting failure? What missionary, especially one from a society whose founders were notable for the depth of their experience of prayer, likes to admit frankly that, despite reading the books recommended for missionaries, he still knows next to nothing about the subject in his own day-to-day experience. He can trot out a few pat answers, but leaves the heart of the matter untouched.

My friend's death forced the matter to the forefront of my mind. And because she was a real person whose memory I cherish, I dare, for her sake, to share my experiences in writing. But be warned! If you want this missionary to remain up in her ivory castle, then read no more . . .

2. CULTURE GAP?

'BUT I couldn't possibly go to a *missionary prayer meeting*!' This comment was repeatedly and emphatically hurled at me during my home leave from Thailand.

The speakers had my sympathy! Guts would be required for a girl in mini-skirt (or one in a cat-suit) and leather boots, or for a young man with shoulder-length hair and strings of beads, to brave the ranks of some such prayer meetings, with formidable arrays of middle-aged, middle-class matrons (or so they appear to some). Having lived as a foreigner in Thailand, and gone through years of hardening so that I no longer minded being culturally different from others around me, I could feel for those who tried to explain why they would feel out of place in an average missionary prayer meeting. Can oil and water mix? Can modern mini-skirts and 'sensible' twin-sets blend together?

Critics of missionary prayer meetings sometimes say that the majority attending are senior citizens; that the male to female ratio is at best one to ten; that the language used for prayer is that of the reign of Queen Elizabeth the First, which they are unable to speak; and that some participants always don hats, which many people no longer possess.

Was it a matter of the generation gap, I wondered?

I loved the elderly ladies, whose prayer groups supported me, and *deeply* appreciated the way in which they took me into their hearts, but I longed for younger people to be ready to take their places in the ranks of those committed to the task of communicating Christ throughout the world.

I found it easy to understand that the whole 'missionary thing' might seem so far out that it was totally irrelevant and unacceptable to some today.

Any concept of unspoilt, uneducated, little black Sambos, waiting longingly on unpolluted 'Africa's coral sands', for a great white preacher to come, topee on head, Bible in hand, standing under palm trees proclaiming the Gospel light to the heathen, was right out! Colonialism, imperialism, white domination, or any kind of racialism was also right out.

But the missionaries of today whom I know are generally quite different from Victorian missionaries. Many are young, up-to-date people whose sole concern is to share Christ in a way that is relevant and meaningful to today's world. Perhaps this was one reason why *I* felt the odd one out at some missionary prayer meetings to which I had been invited as speaker; I was usually the youngest there, hatless, and acutely conscious that perhaps I should have splashed out on more expensive clothes, the hemlines of which would have been ten inches lower than those I had bought cheaply from the chain stores. Neither my outward appearance, nor what I said, always conformed to their image of a missionary. But then I am just an ordinary Christian, called to work overseas.

The privilege of sharing the gospel with the whole world is entrusted by God to the church of all ages: *my* Bible makes no exception of any generation within the twentieth century, neither young nor old. I was sad to meet young people who declared that sharing Christ with the whole world was a Victorian activity. They implied that Jesus' commission to 'make disciples of all nations' had no claims on the obedience of their age-group.

They reasoned something like this: 'Missionaries are old-fashioned Victorian relics; therefore, what they do is a hang-over from Victoriana; therefore, we will have nothing to do with them.'

To which I had to agree that *methods* used by missionaries to present the God Who *is* alive and real today, may *be* or may *have been* out-of-date; but the *motive*, and the call of Jesus Christ, are as relevant now as when Jesus commissioned His first group of followers. It is up to the 'now generation' to share Jesus with its own generation *now*, in *all* parts of the world.

I wanted up-and-coming Christians in England to give this trust of sharing Christ with the rest of the world serious thought; but all too often I was frustrated by their false picture of missionary work.

Hand in hand with this went the fact that the concept of actually *praying for missionaries* seemed very remote and unrelated to the lives of many under-thirties.

Was this only due to the generation gap, I wondered?

I soon had to answer, 'Not always', when I heard about one church in which there flourished both an adult prayer meeting and an exuberant young people's prayer meeting.

'Let's put the two together,' enthused the minister.

'We'd never dare . . . they wouldn't have *us* . . . we'd never fit . . .' responded some of the young Christians, recently off hard drugs.

'Won't it lower the spiritual tone of the meetings?' queried some founder members of the church, tucking worn Bibles under arms.

'Give it a try,' pleaded, and prayed, the minister.

So they did. The experiment proved successful.

Give-and-take was needed on both sides; the young learnt patience, and to appreciate the spiritual maturity behind those lengthy prayer-echoes of the King James version of the Bible; and the older came to love the young, and to realize that their familiar chatty prayers were meaningful, utterly sincere, and surprisingly reverent.

I saw that, although intercessory prayer happened to be practised mainly by older people, it was also practised by some younger people too. They obviously did not regard it as a hang-over from Victorian days. They might confess that they were 'hooked on prayer'.

This set me off exploring the Bible to try and discover when this 'praying-for-other-people' business all began.

If it was relevant to members of that youth group, then perhaps I could find its relevance for me, too.

The search took longer than I anticipated. My Bible was unexpectedly bulging with material on this subject.

3. QUALIFIED TO COMMUNICATE?

PERHAPS my problems started when I was very young.

'Now, children,' echoes my Sunday School teacher's voice down the tunnels of memory. '*This* is Adam!' A paper figure wearing a banana leaf apron or clutching a bunch of flowers, was elevated on to a flannelgraph board.

'Here's Eve!' she said, sticking up a cardboard species of Lady Godiva at his side.

'There they are before the fall,' she pointed to a wall picture of two nude figures gazing demurely into space, from behind a waist-high privet hedge. There were even Easter bunnies hopping around in the foreground.

'This *never* happened!' was my childish reaction to such a presentation. The strategically placed leaves and bushes made me chuckle inwardly. After all, *who* would dress like this?

But such unrealistic visual presentation made me, as a child, doubt the historicity of the story of the Garden of Eden. As I grew older, I was able to recognize what had happened to me. I now believe that there *were* real people in those Old Testament times.

As I follow Jesus' acceptance of the Old Testament as true, I am now able to believe that Old Testament characters *actually lived*. They were as human as I am; they were not mere flannelgraph figures of an artist's imagination.

The characteristic of the first couple in the Bible that made them outstanding to me was their link with God. I found that by modernizing their names I was able to erase the flannelgraph haze which had made them so unreal to me.

I could imagine Pete Adam who was married to Evelyn. This couple was unique because they knew the Almighty Creator God as their best Friend. Regularly, in cool evenings, *God* visited them in their back garden for a Friendly chat. They spent hours with Him, developing their friendship.

I could see that, like me, Pete and Evelyn tended to take friendship for granted, not realizing its great value until it was for ever lost. God had always been their closest Friend; they were on the same wavelength, and went along unquestioningly with His ideas.

When someone put the idea into Evelyn's mind that their Friend might be holding back some benefits from them, she was unsure at first how to react. The idea churned round in her mind, until she began to wonder if it possibly might contain a grain of truth. She tried the idea out on Pete; he was sceptical; but gradually began to wonder. Before long he, too, was doubting their Friend.

She then grasped her opportunity to experiment.

She would act independently, and try doing the one thing that God had forbidden. Not only that, but she made sure that Pete was one with her in this.

They took the plunge, acted off their own bats, and disobeyed God, and their precious friendship with God was shattered. They failed to trust their Friend, and forfeited the close communion previously cherished with God.

I was aware of the fact that the consequences of their action did not stop here. Their declaration of independence was passed on through their children to succeeding generations. They started off a population explosion, which spread mankind throughout the earth: humans estranged from God.

It seemed that, from that time onwards, prayerful communion with God should have been impossible. The picture looked black for mankind. Man had cut himself off from God. But I knew from my own experience that the matter had not been left there. As I read on in the Old Testament, I discovered that rare people were privileged to know God personally. Despite the almost universal rejection of their Creator, a few knew God sufficiently well to hold a conversation with Him.

I immediately began to wonder about these men and women. 'How did *they* achieve this?' 'How were *they* qualified to communicate with God when others couldn't?'

Teaching from way back began to focus gradually in my mind. Finally the answer clicked into place.

'Of course,' I told myself, 'this is all tied up with

those covenants I learnt about in Sunday School and Scripture lessons at school.'

Facts that I already knew began to assume relevance. Because God is the sort of Person that He is, man cannot haphazardly crash his own way into an audience with the Almighty Creator King. To have an audience with this King, a man must have entered through the right channels. The Divine invitation to such an audience with such a King had been proffered, after Adam and Eve's estrangement, by the channel of individual men entering into a covenant relationship with God. This meant that such a man undertook on his part to enter fully into all the privileges and obligations that were part and parcel of being granted such a relationship with God.

The old men, the patriarchs in the early parts of Genesis, had realized the cost of this privilege. They wholeheartedly entered into covenant relationships with God and, as the Bible says, they began to 'call upon the Name of the Lord'.

I was struck again and again by the prayers of some of these men and women of the Old Testament. However, I had to learn to try to stand in their shoes, so that their stories and God's achievements would spring to life for me.

The personality of Abraham hit me with new force. I tried to lift him out of my children's illustrated Bible, and to stop thinking of him as a funny old man in a Victorian nightdress. My husband had recently written an article, signing himself with the pen-name 'Abraham'. So, I let my imagination run riot; suppose my husband *had* been Abraham, and I was Sarah; what would life have been like?

First of all, I would have been married to a very godly man; one who had made many covenants with God, and who knew God more intimately than most people. I could see how frustrated I might get by his persistent quiet assurance that God had promised us a large family; how my frustration over childless years might turn to despair, as I realized that I would never have my own baby; so that I finally persuaded him to produce an heir by intercourse with my personal servant. Yet, Abraham *still* took God at His word. I had been infertile all my life, was now post-menopausal, and it was thirteen years since Abraham's heir had been born to my servant.

Pregnancy was now quite out of the question. Yet, this amazing husband of mine believed God, against all odds . . . and he was right. The impossible happened; we had our first baby in our old age.

That husband of mine lived close enough to God for Him to be able to share the most extraordinary matters with him.

For instance, God shared His grief and concern over the appalling happenings in Sodom and Gomorrah, and His intention to blot out those towns, and stop the spreading destructive rot of their ideas and practices. That husband of mine then had the nerve to plead with God, asking for the towns to be spared because some of our relatives lived there.

Not only did he ask, but God answered his intercession by saving our relatives.

I had to shake myself back to life . . . I was not Sarah, I was myself. Yet my day-dream brought home the fact that Abraham had been amazing in the way in which he had interceded for others. And equally amazing was God's responsiveness.

Now that my mind's ears were tuned in to listen for overtones or faint notes about intercessory prayer, I began to realize that all sorts of people in covenant relationships with God had been communing with Him throughout the Old Testament records. God had patiently listened, and answered their prayers. The examples seemed endless as I began to count them.

'Just pray and God will act? Was that it?' I wondered. 'Not quite.' I was soon to see, when I noticed a peculiar accompaniment to some prayers.

Tucked away in unexpected places in the Old Testament, I discovered that some of these people who prayed were, as the Bible said, 'building altars to the Lord' sometimes, before they 'called upon the Name of the Lord.'

'What's that in aid of?' I had to ask. 'Why are they building up piles of stones on which to sacrifice animals, as neighbouring pagan people do? Have they turned syncretistic, or is there some deep spiritual meaning in it?'

The Thai father of a patient of mine had insisted on returning home one day from hospital. 'Why?' I asked him. 'Because I've promised a sacrifice to the spirits of our house tomorrow, if my son's still alive. I must be home by dawn tomorrow, or my son will die.' (He reached home on time, but his son died later.)

I knew that the God of Creation would never require or accept such a sacrifice. In the Old Testament, sacrifice had many different significances. One meaning was that it was a common way of entering into communion with God. Thus a man was outwardly showing his inner longing to walk with God, and to follow God's way, no matter what it cost. In building altars before they prayed, our forefathers were sometimes saying, 'Almighty God, we are completely Yours, and want every part of ourselves to be what You want.'

In their attitude I found a lesson for myself.

These men would probably have disagreed with John Robinson, who says in *Honest to God*

'I wonder whether Christian prayer, prayer in the light of the Incarnation, is not to be defined in terms of penetration through to the world of God, rather than of withdrawal from the world to God.'

Most of my Christian friends in England would disagree with Bishop Robinson, too. But, having been away from England for four years, I could sense the different climate in some Christian groups from when I had left. Where previously culture and the arts were neglected as worldly, now some Christians were recognizing them as God-given. There was a swing away from the separation of the Christian from activities regarded as 'unspiritual' and towards the involvement of Christians as 'salt' in all aspects of community life. With this swing, there seemed to me to be a swing away from the emphasis on the place of prayer in the life of the Christian and especially away from intercessory prayer.

I could feel the influence of friends as it affected me in my contact with them. Where previously one friend always prayed with us before speaking at a meeting, he no longer did so. Nights spent in prayer, commonplace in my student days, were now exceptional.

My digging in the Old Testament for treasure about intercessory prayer was revealing much that had been buried before. For instance, I had for years been perplexed by Samuel's words 'Far be it from me that I should sin against the Lord by ceasing to pray for you.' (I Samuel 12, verse 23).

A school-friend's name was written beside that verse in my Bible. Every time I turned to it, it was with a pang of conscience 'Twenty or so years . . . and I've *not* been praying for her . . . and it says I've been sinning by my failure.' When ministers hurled this verse as a challenge from the pulpit, as the proof-text that it was sin not to pray for others, I was defenceless and guilty.

However, I began to discover that later on in the Old Testament in the pre-exilic and the prophetic period, intercession was a special ministry, given at this time by God to special people like the prophets, priests and kings. God invested them with the unique right of acting as mediators between God and men; so Samuel *would* have been sinning had he failed to exercise this trust; but this did not *necessarily* apply to *me*.

I heaved a sigh of relief. Why had I felt guilty when preachers proclaimed this verse out of context from their pulpits, '*You've* sinned by failing to pray for others . . . see what the Bible says.' Taken in context, this verse did not always have the meaning attributed to it. God's answers to intercessory prayer in the Old Testament are sometimes miraculous, and embrace both the large and the small details of life. At times it may even appear that man's prayers were powerful enough to force an almighty, omnipotent God to change His mind.

When the Israelites were facing deserved punishment for worshipping the golden calf, God said, 'Now therefore let me alone that my wrath may burn hot against them and I may consume them . . .' (Exodus 32, verse 10). Moses, however, didn't sit quietly and watch his people being destroyed; he pleaded for them ceaselessly, until 'the Lord repented of the evil which he thought to do to His people'. (Exodus 32, verse 14). A similar experience happened to Amos, when he interceded for Jacob, 'The Lord repented concerning this; "This also shall not be," said the Lord God'. (Amos 7, verse 6).

Was this as simple as it sounded? Could I pray, and by my prayers 'twist God's arm', so that He would do whatever I wanted? Jeremiah showed me the impossibility of such a thought. He recorded a time when God went to the extent of forbidding Jeremiah from interceding for the people again, because on this occasion God was going to *have to* punish His children; judgement could be delayed no longer. (Jeremiah 7, verse 16; 11, verse 14; 14, verse 11).

But what was happening, I wondered, when these

men prayed? What happened in the spiritual realm? Someone suggested that it seemed as if God wanted another person to take on the responsibility for the Israelites for a little while, so that He wouldn't have to punish them indefinitely, and repeatedly, for their rebellion against Him.

As far as I was concerned, the whole issue of intercessory prayer was raising more problems than were being solved. I had learnt that intercessory prayer is a very personal experience. It can only be experienced by those who know God for themselves; but a new, thought-provoking element was raising its head; intercessory prayer would only bear fruit if it was in line with God's will.

This has been summed up by Westcott, 'True prayer, the prayer that must be answered, is the personal recognition and acceptance of the divine will. It follows that the hearing of prayer which teaches obedience is not so much the granting of a specific petition which is assumed by the petitioner to be the way to the end desired, but the assurance that what is granted does most effectively lead to the end.'

I knew I was standing on the brink of something important; I had a sinking awareness that to go deeper might lead me to costly action. I was not sure that I was prepared for this.

4. A PRIORITY WITH JESUS

'UNWILLING for costly action' was an attitude that was to make me ashamed for having thought in such a way. I began to look at Jesus and His attitude to prayer.

First of all, I found that I needed to think of Jesus as a real man; not as a pretty picture in the church stained-glass window. He had been a *man*, as well as the Son of God, and the problems and excuses I faced about prayer, He had met Himself and understood perfectly.

Prayer was real and essential to Him. I was staggered to realize the contents of His prayers at times of greatest crises in His life. As He faced the prospect of the torture of His crucifixion, and imagined the agony lying ahead, He did not run away and escape, nor did He collect a supply of opium derivatives to ease His pain. He looked the issues squarely in the face, and went away to pour out His heart in prayer to God. The fact that gripped me was that, at such a time as this, not only did He pray for Himself, but His prayer focused on others . . . right down to a twentieth century Christian *like me*. As His friend, John, tells us, Jesus' prayer was, 'I do not pray for these only, but also for those who are to believe in Me through their word.' (John 17, verse 20). At His time of bitter crisis, Jesus prayed *for me*. Even while He was slowly dying up on the Cross, He not only prayed for Himself, but He included in His prayers those who were responsible for His death, seeking God's forgiveness for them.

This Man knew how to pray for other people, and obviously gave it high priority in His life. My first excuse would be, 'Well, I just haven't got time.' But I couldn't plead, 'He had plenty of time, while I haven't', because this wouldn't be true.

If ever a man was mobbed by his fellow-men, it was Jesus. It seems that someone was always after Him for some kind of help. My reaction to a non-stop day in the hospital is to collapse thankfully into bed, and if I pray at all at this stage, it is to pray that the 'phone won't go calling me out of bed to go to a patient in need of help. Not so with Jesus. He possessed the love that not only gave time to help people practically, but also found time to commune with God and to intercede for them.

And, honestly, some of my excuses for not praying for others must seem more than feeble excuses to God. Could I ever face His judgement seat, and if asked why I had failed to exercise intercessory prayer, reply, 'Well, there's the TV, and I like to watch it most evenings; I have to give time to painting the house and doing up the furniture; and to keeping the garden presentable, and exercising the dog . . . and so on.'

I can imagine my eyes being unwilling to meet God's as I make my attempts at excuses, knowing only too well that 'no time' is really a cover-up for time that has been frittered away, and wasted on trivialities.

The Jesus I profess to love and follow said, 'It is enough for the disciple to be like his teacher, and the servant like his master . . .' (Matthew 10, verse 25). He also said, 'As the Father has sent Me, even so I send you.' (John 20, verse 21).

I have no reason to deduce that these statements of Jesus, referring to me, exclude intercessory prayer.

It is of such importance to Him that the Bible says that He is still praying for other people, 'He always lives to make intercession for them' (Hebrews 7, verse 25).

I had experienced prayer (at its rarest, highest best) as both an indefinable mystical communion with an indescribably great God, and as co-ordination and healing of my whole personality, so that I desired to live as God wanted me to. Now I find that this is only one facet; I have never flipped the coin of prayer over to look at the other side. Prayer is not solely concerned with me and my life; my prayer is to be equally concerned with the lives of other people.

Jesus taught His followers a prayer, which is so familiar to me that it has lost its meaning. It has become a sacred jumble of sentences, learnt in childhood, and repeated as a ritual many times every Sunday. As I study it afresh I am struck by something glaring me in the face, that I have failed to see all my life.

It was a simple fact that I should have noticed before, had the 'Lord's Prayer' not become a part of the Church of England service which I find it easy to drift through; mouth-mumbling formulae memorized in childhood; mind wandering everywhere, rarely truly worshipping. All my life I had been saying, 'Thy kingdom come, Thy will be done on earth as it is in heaven' *before* 'Give us this day our daily bread'.

Prayer for the establishment of God's Kingdom in our world precedes prayer for me, and my daily needs. Yet, in my personal prayer time I tend to place me and my needs first; others come second, are just tagged on as a kind of P.S. at the end, or are completely left out.

I was becoming increasingly uncomfortable about my brand of praying. It was getting more apparent that it was far from what it should be. Praying for others was, for me, a kind of optional-extra often omitted for various reasons.

I knew that the early church gave it high priority. Paul's letters made me ashamed. He knew how to intercede in depth for newly-emerging churches, struggling to maturity. He was even able to say in complete honesty to the Colossian Church, 'We have not ceased to pray for you.'

Dare I admit the truth to such an emerging church, I would have to confess, 'I've never started to pray deeply for you.' Or perhaps, 'I used to pray for you, but I'm afraid I've lost heart, lost interest, lost touch and lost enthusiasm . . . And to be honest, my favourite TV programme takes preference over intercessory prayer for you. You wouldn't want me to miss a weekly series for you, would you?'

This was a bitter pill for me to swallow, especially as I wore the label 'full-time missionary', and this is not the kind of admission expected from a missionary.

I was confronted by the truth: Jesus and the early church placed priority on intercessory prayer . . . I had not.

I was next confronted by the question, 'What's it all about? Why does God want us to carry out such a practice? Surely an omnipotent God doesn't need *me* to pray, before He can move into a life or a situation . . . What is there to this business?'

5. JUST A MATHEMATICAL EQUATION?

THE ad. I might have inserted in the personal columns of the newspaper would have read,

'Wanted: One tame Theologian . . . who speaks plain English.'

Most theologians used a language which made me refer constantly to a theological dictionary. Some books I tackled which dealt with intercessory prayer left me more confused than before. Why wouldn't someone speak simply? I knew that if I could only digest the meat served up by some of these theologians, I would find the answers to many of my questions.

Then, right at the time when I needed a person who spoke ordinary everyday language, God gave me the gift of the contact with a theologian. This man spoke in non-theological terms: *I* could understand him. He also did not appear to think it in the least unusual, or unnecessary, to be sitting on the floor shivering in a corridor late one night at a conference, sorting out one missionary's theological problems. His generosity with his time, and his interest, gave me the courage to write and ask him,

'*Why* does an almighty, omnipotent God *need* someone like *me* to intercede for other men . . . surely such a God can get along and act perfectly well without my having to pray and ask Him to?'

His reply came by return post, 'God enables sinful men to enter a little into His creative purposes for the world, to enrol in the struggle (of which the outcome is assured by the resurrection) of bringing His will to be done on earth as it is in Heaven.

'Prayer is participating with God in His work, is it not? This is the primary meaning of it all; petition, confession, and even thanksgiving are all subordinate to this . . . Why should God need me to pray? . . . He doesn't *need*. But He does *want* my fellowship, my sharing in the work, my constant expression (by the very fact of prayer) of dependence.'

I read and re-read those words. A dim light began to glow, gradually brightening to a blaze illuminating a new aspect of truth for me.

I wanted to shout out loud, 'God doesn't *need*, He *wants*!'

God wanted me to share in His work throughout the world by my praying; and such praying expressed my need of God, and my dependence on Him to move into those lives and situations for which I prayed.

A saying, often quoted, made sense for the first time, 'Don't say, "I'm praying for the work" because prayer *is* the work!' I had regarded this previously as a sop to the conscience of those who should be 'working' but couldn't be bothered to; or as a tranquillizer for those who wanted to be doing 'the work', but for some reason were not able to.

I had inwardly half agreed with the cynic who

challenged me at a student meeting, 'Sitting on your bottom praying is the laziest way out of helping someone that I can think of!'

I still agreed with the cynical student that costly action was called for in many situations; but I was now beginning to see that prayer *also* merited a place in helping others in their needs.

A medical student had cottoned on to this when he shared with me his thoughts about intercessory prayer: I believe that being a Christian is the same in some ways as being called to be a missionary. When I realized this, and was willing to be involved in God's plan for this world, I then saw that right now I can be part of a team of missionaries . . . God can unite me with a missionary, in a fellowship of prayer, so that instead of one person working out there, there are now two.'

This fact that God wants men to share in His work in the world by their prayers has sometimes (probably unintentionally and unthinkingly) been twisted to produce all kinds of false ideas. We may find ourselves thinking:

'God didn't work in this situation; He couldn't because we failed to pray sufficiently. After all, Jesus said, "Ye have not because ye ask not." '

Yet we need to determine exactly in what we place our trust. Do we place our trust *in God*, or is it *in the power of our prayers*? If it is in prayer itself, then we find prayer becomes a peculiar mechanical means through which we try to obtain our desired end.

We may even think in terms of 'plugging into God'

to receive 'charging of our spiritual batteries' and 'sufficient power' for a certain situation. We may take it further and assume that the longer we 'plug in' then the more power we will automatically receive.

On this basis, all-night prayer meetings are a more speedy, efficient means of producing a desired end than a few minutes of intensive deep fellowship with God in intercession at mid-day.

Such false reasoning can lead us on to propose that 'The more people I can get to pray for this situation, the more quickly God can act.'

It may lead us even further, '*I'll try* harder. I so long to see God move in this situation that *I'll try* fasting as well as praying.'

For some of us, fasting may have more to do with slimming than with praying! Yet it has been hallowed by centuries of Christians as a means of enabling them to detach themselves from their physical needs, and to focus their whole beings intensely on God alone, and thus experience a depth of fellowship with Him that they might otherwise never achieve. I found it interesting to learn that, in the King James version of the New Testament, prayer and fasting are linked together sometimes. However, more recent translations leave out 'fasting', because it is believed this word was added to later manuscripts, as the early church experienced the value of fasting; the word is not thought to have appeared in the original manuscripts.

We sometimes distort the legitimate, good use of fasting, that of concentrated communion with God;

and turn it into an action which is like trying to 'twist God's arm' and 'make' Him act, which renders nonsense our Christian concept of an omnipotent, Creator God. We reduce Him to the stature of a marionette, which only moves when *we* pull the right strings.

Although intercessory prayer is vital, we must beware of false motives and false assumptions. I might like to try mentally to reduce intercessory prayer to an arithmetical equation like this:

God + Prayers (me + x number of others) = Desired Answer.

But to do so would be denying the true character of God.

Much as I, an existential human being, would like to, I cannot deny that there is a deep element of mystery in intercessory prayer; nor dare I try to reduce the immensity of God to that which my finite mind can grasp and completely understand.

A mystery remains, and a paradox exists. I see that the omnipotent, almighty God, *does* sometimes seem to answer all-night-long prayers; He *does* sometimes answer prayer coupled with fasting; and He *does* sometimes answer the prayers of the many, where the prayers of a few appear to go unanswered. However, these answers come from a God who is loving and gracious . . . . They do not come because the pray-ers have *earned* the right to be granted their wishes. The omnipotent God remains free to act, or not to act, according to His will, whether or not we pray.

I was aghast, as a new, idealistic missionary, to

discover that God had *not* answered the prayers (or so it seemed on the face of things) of about a hundred Overseas Missionary Fellowship *missionaries*, working in Central Thailand. They had covenanted to pray that 1,000 Thai people would become Christians within three years.

My husband and I arrived on the scene in the middle of the three years.

We waited expectantly to see 1,000 Christians blossoming forth . . . after all, all those *missionaries* praying must surely merit God's answering their intercessions . . . . Yet a mere handful braved the uprooting from their Buddhist heritage to confess their Christian faith openly in baptism. No-one said anything to us, the new missionaries, about the fact that prayer had apparently gone unanswered. Our idealism and hope tarnished slightly. I was slow to learn that while God's Word is true, and 'the effective fervent prayer of a righteous man availeth much', this does not automatically assure that God will answer both in the manner and within the time-limits set by the intercessors. Yet I now possess sufficient courage to believe that at some time in the future God *is* going to answer the prayers of those hundred missionaries (if He has not done so, secretly, already).

Knowing that God did not *need* me to intercede, but that He *wanted* me to, gave me both fresh perspective and fresh insight into intercessory prayer.

It was as if God had left a door slightly open, and was saying, 'Come on in and share this with Me, if you want to . . . you don't *have to*, but I'd treasure your co-operation and unity in this . . .'.

Yet for years I had not noticed the door was ajar, nor heard God's invitation; then, having noticed and heard, I had failed to understand. Now I was without excuse, and could no longer plead ignorance.

What would I do with God's invitation? Was I going to be among the indifferent?

Or was I, with an indignant, deliberate shove, going to slam this door shut in God's face? 'No thanks, God! Your offer's appreciated . . . but this time it's asking a bit much . . . intercessory prayer isn't my kind of thing . . . it's all right for George Mullers and Hudson Taylors . . . it's not for me in the twentieth century!'

6.   THE ENEMY

THE response of a bull to a red rag is insignificant compared with the reaction of a certain family when one member defiantly refers to 'the devil' as a 'personal being'. For another member immediately blasts off rockets aimed at destroying once and for all any lingering and supposedly medieval concept of a figure with horns, tail and pitchfork.

I have no intention here of entering at length into this dispute; nor of trying to define the devil in terms which our twentieth century minds can grasp; nor of grappling with conflicting concepts of what the devil really is. I am aware that, as C. S. Lewis and others have stated, one of the devil's cleverest tricks is to try to persuade men that there is no such thing as a devil.

However, the Bible makes it very clear that there *is* a struggle going on in the spiritual realm between the good, loving Creator God, and the power of evil. The devil, who is a person, is striving to ruin and destroy the work of this loving Creator God.

There is constant conflict between the devil and God, about which we humans are rarely aware.

I know from experience that this is happening; but am often only conscious of the struggle in retrospect.

For instance, I have been foolish enough to write articles or stories about Thai Christians; I have 'pooh-poohed' those who have warned me that by writing of these people I am making them sitting targets for the devil's attacks . . . yet, this is apparently *exactly* what *has* happened. Two Christians whose lives I recorded were severely tested at the time of publication of their stories, and both gave in to the hard temptations they faced. By putting them in the public eye like this, I *had* exposed them to enemy attack. I was forced to admit that I was wrong to have been sceptical; the devil *had* aimed his attacks hard and strong at them after my writings; and I was partly responsible for their fall.

Similarly, in the hospital where I work often we are conscious of the struggle going on between God and the evil one. Patients long to turn to the loving, living Christian God, but the devil holds them in the grip of fear that if they tear off their spirit strings, and the amulets from around their necks, then something terrible will happen to them.

If we agree that intercessory prayer is sharing with God in His work in the world, then we may be able to accept the concept that intercessory prayer has a part to play in defeating the power of the evil one. I believe that there are some people for whom we have a special responsibility to pray. If I now write about individual Thai Christians, I feel that because *I* have placed them in the devil's firing-line, *I* personally am responsible to pray for them.

I am responsible to accept God's invitation to share

in His work in their lives, of deflecting the bullets of the evil one, and of enabling them to emerge all the stronger and maturer for their testing. As a writer, I am responsible to pray for those about whom I write.

I also believe that churches have a similar responsibility for those whom they have sent overseas, as their representatives, as missionaries.

The young new missionary recruit often sends out so-called 'prayer cards', which show his photo, often with an ethereal haze around his head and a visionary fire in his eye. But does his church know what it is sending him to? I know from experience that he is being sent straight into the front-line of the battle between God and the devil. I am so grateful for the two groups of individuals in my own church who accept prayer responsibility for me, as I am so often aware of being ceaselessly attacked by one tactic of the devil after another.

A young missionary from my church on her first leave home wrote, 'If folk at home don't pray for me, then I'd better stay at home! My reaction to my first term of service is that the missionfield is like a fierce battlefield, in which there are no cease-fires. In an ordinary war, ground soldiers are not expected to fight unless sufficient air cover is provided; otherwise they might soon be wiped out.

'Constant overhead protection and reinforcements are vital. Any country sending troops into ground battle without such support might justly be accused of condemning these men to defeat and death.

'Similarly, it seems to me to be equally irresponsible

for a church to send someone out as its representative into the warfare of the missionfield, if that church is unable or unwilling to maintain sufficient, continual praying forces to defeat the enemy attacks that strike missionaries continually.'

Knowing how grateful I am for those in my home church who feel responsible to pray for me, because *I am their representative in Thailand*, I covet this for all my missionary friends.

Some have no churches with the responsibility of praying for them.

The devil's main aim with missionaries (as with any Christians) is somehow to get and keep them out of touch with God and to render them ineffective or inactive in their lives as Christians, so that people looking at them will be unimpressed. The devil can do his best to get a missionary removed by death, or by return home: or he can try and make sure that this missionary's presence abroad will either be a hindrance to others, or be so innocuous that it counts for nothing. He has then scored a major triumph.

However, it is not so easy for him, for God already has the upper hand through Calvary's victory. As Henry Martyn said, 'While God has work for me to do, I cannot die!' There was evidence of the truth of this in a letter I received from an O.M.F. single lady missionary living alone in the Philippines:

'In the summer of 1954 I went to work on my own amongst the Iraya tribe. They provided me with a small house that was not in use at the back of their village. There were only a few banana leaves for walls, and a little porch at one end. Each night, according to custom, they sent two children to sleep with me.

'After a time some of these people accepted the gospel, but there were several who opposed it. They were mainly men, who seemed to enjoy going to the town and returning drunk. Usually they just passed by the house on the main trail to the village, and although we heard their loud talking we were never troubled. I always prayed that they would eventually come to trust the Lord.

'One day an official in the town asked all the men in the village to go and help with some jobs he wanted done. In the afternoon, the mothers of the two children who slept in my house informed me that they needed the children to stay at home, as their husbands were away. I understood, and said I did not mind staying alone, provided they approved. So that night I was alone in my little house.

'During the night I heard loud talking and laughing. As the drunken men approached the house, I could clearly hear the words,

'"Let's kill her!"'

'"We'll see if there's a God!"'

'"Kill her . . ."'

'I sat up in bed praying for the men. My heart was pounding, as I wondered who was their intended victim. They came closer, but suddenly as they reached the path leading to my house, there was no more sound from them, until at a distance I could hear them having a subdued discussion in the centre of the village.

'The following morning, two of the older ladies who had recently become Christians came to visit me. They asked if I had been afraid the previous night when the men passed by. I told them that I had woken up, and had been praying for both the men and for my own safety.

'They told me that one of the men wanted to kill me: but as he went to turn down the path leading to my house, his way was blocked by two men in white who were standing there. He was frightened and went home to tell the others what he had seen.

'I told the women that the men must have been God's angels, sent to protect His child.

'Not long afterwards I received a letter from my mother, saying that she had woken up one night and felt compelled to pray for my safety. The following morning she was 'phoned by a friend, a prayer-partner of mine, saying that she too had woken up that night and felt compelled to pray for me, believing me to be in danger.

'On checking the dates I found that this was the very night that the man had wanted to kill me'.

As with Job in the Old Testament, God would not allow this missionary to be killed; and He allowed two who prayed for her to share in His work of protecting her that dangerous night.

I find it comforting to know that literally 'my times are in His hands'; God will keep me alive as long as He wants. 'Man is immortal until his work is done' are words that have given me courage in some situations which, on a human level, might have led to fatal accidents.

While I am assured that the devil cannot easily get rid of me by killing me off, I still find myself asking questions like,

'Can he remove me or render me ineffective by so manipulating the stresses and strains of missionary life that I become mentally sick, and unable to function properly?'

'How far will God permit the devil to go in my life? Where does God draw the line, and command, "So far . . . no further!" as He did for Job?'

And God gives me no clear-cut answer except for the assurance that He has an overwhelming depth of love for me, and cares what happens to me.

'What part do the prayers of other people play in all this?', I find myself wondering. Questions galore flood my mind.

There was a story going round, from preacher to preacher, about a missionary of the China Inland Mission, who was in China some years ago. One night he was protected from robbery, because the bandit who was planning to rob him was scared away by a band of twelve guards surrounding the missionary. In reality the missionary was alone. It so happened, that at that exact moment of time, exactly twelve people were at a prayer meeting in England praying for this missionary. Every version of this story always concluded like this:

'Supposing only five people had been praying . . . or only one . . . or none at all . . .' Culminating with a deduction, a challenge and an appeal for intercession for missionaries, 'That missionary might have been killed!'

(I found this story, which was told by different people, very difficult to trace. It appears in many versions, with different numbers of people praying in each version . . . but a story *can* be found in one of the old C.I.M. books.)

This story nagged at me for months. While I could thank God for those who shared His protection of this missionary by their prayers, was I *really* to presume, as preachers sometimes wanted me to, that an omnipotent God was *not* strong enough, or had limited Himself and could *not* protect someone, *unless* He was strengthened by people's prayers? Was I further to conclude that the degree of protection He was able to provide was limited by the number of those praying? Is God's power like a type of concrete, that will only stand strain if reinforced by the steel of intercessory prayer?

'For I, the Lord your God, hold your right hand; it is I who say to you "Fear not, I will help you".' When God made this promise to *me* as a new missionary, He did not make His promise of help provisional on my finding those who would pray for me.

Next, a pastor shared with me his experiences of a girl who had gone abroad from his church as a missionary.

'It was tragic,' he said, 'Things went well at first, and then considerable tension arose between her and others. She didn't know how to write and explain it all to friends at home, and was very unhappy. Yet it was one of those matters in which love and prayer would have made all the difference.

'As it was, we at home knew nothing about it. She lasted only a year and a half, and then had to come home . . . I'm sure that the whole area of intercessory prayer is far wider and more potent than we generally realize.'

In other words, he seemed to be saying, 'If only we'd known and prayed, then everything would have been right, and we wouldn't have had a "missionary casualty" on our hands.'

I began to wonder if I could make out a case of cause and effect from examples like this, which is one of many similar true examples.

Could I deduce no prayer for another Christian (cause) leads to inevitable failure (effect)? I tried this theory out on a missionary doctor, asking about the relationship between prayer and mental breakdowns in some missionaries.

She replied, 'I worked out seven factors, of which if more than two existed then the likelihood of breakdown seemed to increase . . . My opinion would be that if a missionary had, say, two factors against him (e.g. a disturbed home background, and a rigid personality which found it hard to adapt to change) then the presence or absence of a praying group might be the factor that tipped the balance for success or failure as a missionary . . . I know of one case where there was no group praying at home, and that missionary is no longer on the field.'

On the other hand a Christian psychiatrist gave me a

different view-point, 'I'm sure it isn't fair to suggest that mental breakdowns are being started off all the time . . . or that if they do occur, they are *ipso facto* evidence that no one has cared enough or that no one has prayed enough.

'Wouldn't that really suggest God's hand is not strong enough, that our health depends *only* on the prayers, or the involvement, of others? That's to say, it might be possible to over-emphasize the place of intercessory prayer in preventing breakdowns. I don't know what *evidence* I can put forward that prayer prevents breakdowns, though I *may believe* that it has *something* to do with it *sometimes*.'

At this point I had reached an impasse, and was none the wiser because of the conflicting views. I remained bewildered until I finally began to look at intercessory prayer from a new angle.

The fact that I pray expresses my dependence on God. This works out in the realm of my own prayers for myself. But I began to see that I could carry this principle of dependence one step further, into my praying for others. In praying for them, I am expressing my dependence on God to do something for them in their lives and situations. God desires such expressions of dependence.

With this realization comes a deep sense of the mystery of intercessory prayer. An omnipotent God cannot be compressed to the size that my finite mind can fully comprehend. I can never know all the answers. Yet a battle is going on between God and the evil one: my part in the battle in the lives of others is to pray for them. I have a responsibility to pray for other people. Neglect to intercede will not directly hurt me; but my failure to pray may lead to insufficient protection for someone who is vulnerable and in the direct target area for the devil's incoming mortar bombs.

I need prayerfully to ask God which people I am especially responsible to pray for.

Dare I shrug and cheerfully say, 'I'm O.K. Jack!' and by my neglect leave another in danger of being hurt?

7. THE GOD OF THE IMPOSSIBLE

WHETHER we like it or not, Jesus said it:

'Remain in union with me, and I will remain in union with you. Unless you remain in union with me, you cannot bear fruit . . . for you can do nothing without me.' He states this very plainly. (John 15, verses 4-5, TEV).

'But Jesus . . .' we try answering back, 'You don't really mean what you're saying, do You? Surely, You must mean that as long as we're new Christians we're to depend on You, as a baby depends on its father. Once we're adolescents, we can spread our wings a bit, can't we? Shouldn't we become *less* dependent, just as a human child grows to maturity and becomes independent of its parents? Isn't this the reason you sometimes give new Christians highly dramatic answers to prayer, while the rest of us see little obvious reponse for all our prayers?'

Back re-echoes the word of Jesus, unchanging, '*You can do nothing without me!*' His words are reinforced by the life which He lived; He was dependent on God His Father to work in and through Him. Reading John's Gospel, I lost count of just how many times Jesus expressed His dependence on God for everything. Was this the point at which I sometimes took the wrong turning in my praying—lacking a sense of helplessness, and dependence on God? Human pride makes us reluctant to admit that without our God we can achieve nothing of lasting value.

Do we, for convenience, pretend that Jesus never said those words expressing our need of Him?

A missionary stuck in the hills of North Thailand had come to the end of her resources and shared with me the way God got her out of an impossible situation.

'My colleague and I were cooling off in a shady spot in the middle of the jungle. We were on our way to help a sick missionary. We had already trekked five hours but were still a long way from Palm Leaf village, our destination. We did not know the trail and so were dependent on the old opium smoker, our carrier and guide. Then right there, miles from anywhere, he decided he could go no further. Nothing would budge him.

'We needed to have our medicines and food carried. We needed a guide. It was vital to get to Palm Leaf village that day.

'God had promised, "My God shall supply all your need." Did He fulfil His promise?

'We sat there praying in the middle of the jungle. As we prayed and pondered, up the trail lumbered the biggest answer to prayer that I've ever seen: a great grey, ear-flapping elephant.

'Who but God could have arranged such perfect timing?

'The elephant was even heading for Palm Leaf village

to haul logs there, and its driver kindly agreed to transport our baggage. Our hearts lightened, and with this so did our carrier's load. So much so, that he perked up immediately, and guided us for the rest of our journey.'

Someone was driven to a point of helplessness, and at this level God was able to meet her need, even with such an extraordinary answer to prayer as an elephant.

I began to think about some of our prayer meetings and times of prayer alone with God. We sit, or occasionally kneel, often with a list of labelled prayer topics, and dutifully work through the list from top to bottom, mentioning each person or subject in its turn.

. . . *a worthy exercize and not to be discarded lightly*. But is this really all that God wants of us? Are we letting ourselves off too lightly? The exercise of working through a list of prayer topics may for some be a misguided attempt to try to inject God's power into the vein of an individual's soul; a sort of spiritual shot in the arm, to pep him up a bit. We neither feel helpless in the face of human need, nor powerless to act in a situation, to the extent that we are forced to come crying to God as a last resort, 'God, without You this whole thing is a terrible mess!' So called 'shopping list' praying tends to lack any element of human need.

This lack is one reason why some of our attempts at intercession may seem barren and mechanical at times. Our prayer topics for the day, which we have jotted down, may not include anything for which we sense any need to come to God in desperation.

We dutifully pray for Evangelist Successful, when

deep down we are assured that E.S.'s forthcoming campaign in our town is 'bound to be successful' because he always is. We pray for E.S.'s campaign because we have been taught that this is expected of us; but we lack the assurance that unless God works through E.S., by His Holy Spirit, the whole thing will flop; perhaps this is why many pre-campaign prayer meetings are poorly attended. 'If E.S. is automatically going to succeed, then why bother praying about it?' This may be the unspoken assumption of some Christians. Our very lack of dependence on God, expressed by lack of prayer, may result in E.S.'s campaign *not* being a success.

But we don't like admitting that, and see that the report in the religious press says that 'We are sure a lasting work must have been done . . .'

We can then carry this attitude through to our praying for individuals. After reading a certain missionary's prayer letters someone remarked, 'He always sounds so holy that I feel it's *me* who needs the prayer; not *him*'. This pray-er knew of no situation in that missionary's life which he could bring to God in desperation for God to act and change things.

God delights to respond to our cries of human need. Recently I was aware of what, in human terms, was a hopeless situation. It seemed that the conflicting and strongly-held principles of several missionaries might lead to the resignation of valued workers. Hours were spent talking over the situation; others of us who knew, but were not involved in the situation, spent many hours praying. Humanly speaking, the situation was hopeless, and there seemed nothing that man could do to alter the state of affairs. Then God took over, and a quiet miracle began. Strong principles are still held strongly; but God cemented in the bond of His love those who were separated. Now instead of a volcanic eruption of personality clash, God miraculously has lovingly united the people who formerly had little understanding of one another, other than their common desire to follow God's will.

I can continue to pray for those involved, knowing that, apart from God's restraining hand, the bomb might yet erupt in destruction one day. However, I have seen God de-fuse this bomb in answer to prayer offered in a situation of utter frustration at our inability to do anything on the human level.

However, learning to pray in helplessness is only half of what I need to grasp; I also need to understand in earnest how to pray with faith. It basically makes sense. What is the point of praying, if I don't really believe God will, or can, do anything?

Christians sometimes declare, 'Our God is the God of the impossible'.

I am challenged, 'Do I believe Him to be so? What about the impossible situation I face today in my own life; in the church; in the office; in the government; in the moral corruption of my country; in the pollution of God's world . . . can or will God respond to my prayers about these matters?'

'What about suffering Christians in Communist countries; thousands starving to death across the world; major political issues of our age . . . can my prayers make any contribution?'

It seems crystallized in the question, 'Do I believe that God is big enough and powerful enough, and that He works when I pray?'

It takes courage to accept Jesus' words literally, and then to live them daily. He says, 'If you believe, you will receive whatever you ask for in prayer.' (Matthew 21, verse 22, TEV).

Yet, as I ask God for enough courage to take Him at His word and believe that He *can* answer; that He is *powerful enough*, I have to remember that He rarely answers by breaking the laws of Nature which He has organized, and through which His world operates. Nor does He override the free will given to man and the consequences of man choosing wrongly, unless there is an exceptional reason for this.

I cannot *expect* God to act miraculously, although I know that He sometimes may.

I heard a fascinating story of God's answer to prayer when men believed Him, and accepted the fact that there was nothing they could do themselves.

'In the summer about fifteen years ago, the Overseas Missionary Fellowship and the Sudan United Mission both suffered a severe shortage of income. It happened that a wealthy Yorkshireman had died, and left a large sum of money to be divided between these two societies. However, the money could not be made available until a decision had been made on the will by the Chancery Court in London.

'The Solicitor acting for both Societies was a personal friend of mine.

'He knew that if the case was not heard before the end of July, then there would be no chance of a decision before October (and financial shortage meant that the missionaries needed the money in the summer, if they were going to have enough to live on). Mid-July came and there were still two or three cases ahead, so he asked the Clerk of Court if the case was likely to be reached before the vacation.

'The Clerk replied, ''No. The Judge concerned is slow, and the cases ahead of yours are complicated. It would need a miracle.''

'The word, ''miracle'' came to the Solicitor like a challenge, and he quickly replied, ''Well, my clients are missionary societies, I know that God does miracles in answer to their prayers; so I'll ask them to pray for this miracle!''

'The Clerk laughed, ''Don't believe in miracles myself . . . but if your case is heard before the vacation, then I might change my views!''

'The Solicitor went back to his office. He telephoned the O.M.F. and S.U.M. headquarters, asking them to focus prayer on the matter, and then turned to other matters as he felt there was no more he could do.

'Quite soon he was interrupted by a telephone call from the Clerk, who asked, ''Have your clients started praying yet?''

' ''About half an hour ago. Why?''

' ''An extraordinary thing has happened,'' came the Clerk's reply, ''The Lord Chief Justice has just rung to say that he's been looking at my lists of cases awaiting a hearing, and has decided to put on an additional judge to get the list cleared before the vacation. Your case will be heard next Monday morning.''

' ''Will this change your attitude to prayer?'' the Solicitor asked.

' ''It has certainly made me believe in the effectiveness of your client's prayers . . . I've never known anything like this happen before . . . it's quite extraordinary!'' '

A true story like this makes me face some issues squarely.

Jesus said, 'You can do nothing without me.' Do I believe this or not?

Am I willing to forfeit my prized, proud independence and learn to lean on Him for everything if I am going to accept His words?

Jesus also said, 'If you believe, you will receive whatever you ask for in prayer.' Do I believe like this or not?

If I say, 'Yes, Lord, I believe . . . please help my unbelief,' then I cannot run away from the question, *Then why don't I pray more?*

8.   INSTANT EVERYTHING

'You can't possibly spend so many hours just preparing food!' I almost exclaimed out loud to a Thai friend.

I felt mildly annoyed as I watched her painstakingly chopping, by hand, bits of chicken, pork and vegetables into tiny pieces; carefully and patiently adding exactly the right quantities of spices and curries; and even bothering to sculp some root vegetables into minute delicate shapes. All this labour was on behalf of her family's *normal* evening meal; hours of work which would be demolished in a matter of minutes.

My mind flew to a kitchen I knew in England, full of packets of deep-frozen, ready-prepared meals; freeze-dried foods, and instant soups and puddings. I had to admit that my outlook on life tended to be one of instant everything whilst that of Thai friends usually was a patient, persistent and gentle means of obtaining the same end-result. Up-country where I lived, people had never heard of instant foods, instant car-washes, instant shoe shines, instant floor cleaners, etc; and if they did might possibly see little point in them . . . after all, it is an acquired art to learn the Thai skill of polishing floors with only water, cloth and rubbing, to produce the shine.

Our differences in attitude came home afresh as I examined the way in which I prayed. As I waded through books on intercessory prayer, written in earlier centuries, I became increasingly aware that these saintly Christians of former eras were not *me*.

I never prayed as they had; in particular, I knew nothing in experience of that 'wrestling in prayer' and that 'persistent, unremitting plea to God which refuses to take "no" for an answer' of which they wrote. We were poles apart.

I suspect that I have been so geared and conditioned to a life of instant everything, and to a life packed brim-full by activity, that I have failed to give serious thought to how much priority should be given to prayer.

This made me dig deeper into the Bible. What *was* this wrestling in prayer about which Christians of former centuries wrote?

My immediate reaction was to think of a doctor's mess in an English hospital on a Saturday afternoon, when most doctors were engrossed in all-in wrestling matches on the TV which held no appeal to female me. Two men struggling, their bodies twisting, turning, and trapping; one pinned down, immobilized, and the other the victor . . . what *was* the point?

Was this what God and Jacob had been up to in Genesis chapter 32, and if so what had been the point of it? I had heard this account spiritualized by various preachers, but could not ignore a fact which emerged, which cannot be written off in purely spiritual terms;

the Bible makes it clear that Jacob's hip was dislocated, as a result of his encounter with the wrestler. Despite the severe pain of a hip injury, Jacob continued struggling with the wrestler; he refused to release his hold until his request was granted; and he received the blessing from God he so desired.

This experience was of such a quality that Jacob confesses that during that struggle he encountered God face-to-face: no greater blessing could be bestowed on any human, even if received at the price of pain.

The New Testament mentions a Canaanite woman who came to Jesus begging for His mercy to be shown by His healing her sick child. Jesus responded by silence. His disciples, fed up with the woman trailing around behind them making a nuisance of herself by her persistence, asked Jesus to get rid of her Himself. He replied that, sure enough, His call *was* to the Jews, implying not to the Canaanites. Yet the woman *still* would not leave them alone, and fought back in return by a battle of wits and words, in a frontal encounter with Jesus Himself. Her determination and faith won; Jesus immediately healed her daughter.

I did not know what to make of these two incidents. Superficially, it seemed mean of God not to have answered Jacob's prayer without first dislocating his hip and deforming him for life; and it seemed heartless of Jesus to have put the anguished Canaanite mother through the mill as He did. However, closer scrutiny made me realize that the end-result was that God was able to do far more for these two than they had originally dared request. Jacob asked only for God's blessing; yet he was privileged in being allowed to encounter God personally. The Canaanite woman asked only for healing of her daughter; yet her experience of testing produced a very deep faith in Jesus that would be precious for ever to her.

Was I missing something?

My rushed 'God, please help . . .' could never by any exaggerated stretch of my imagination be called 'wrestling with God'. Did God sometimes want *me* to 'wrestle in prayer' for myself, someone else, or some situation, in order that He might through such an experience give me life-long treasure that would be indescribably precious? I had a hunch that He did, and that consequently I was failing to receive some of the riches He wanted to shower on me.

The shallowness of my praying is challenged. I wonder if some of us today lack the spiritual depth of Christians of former eras because we fail to go deep with God. The quality of human relationships are often directly proportional to the time spent cultivating them; similarly the growth of our knowledge of God as a real person can be stunted by failure to give adequate time to developing this relationship.

Jesus tells two stories indicating His views on the manner in which we should be praying. As is the custom in Thailand, a whole family was tucked up in one bed, settled for the night, all soundly asleep. As a mother, I know that if my three children were in bed with me, then the last thing I would want would be for a neighbour to thud on the door and shout out, loudly asking for food to feed an unexpected guest. I could imagine the scene only too well; everyone would wake up, the children would want drinks, the baby would cry and it would take some time to restore peace. Yet the neighbour persistently knocked until there was nothing for it, his friend had to risk waking the children and get up and give him the food he requested.

Jesus also tells another story about a wronged widow, who pestered the life out of a judge until he finally settled for a quiet life, and saw that she had justice, and left him alone in peace.

I find these two fascinating stories open to mis-interpretation. Is Jesus saying that God is an unwilling friend, who'll only be bothered to help if we make thorough nuisances of ourselves? Or is He saying that God is an unjust judge, not bothering to see that justice is done until forced to?

Of course Jesus is *not* saying this.

Jesus here is talking about *prayer* and not describing God's character. He does *not* say that God is to be equated with either the unwilling friend or the unjust judge. Jesus is trying to get us to see that, although God answers all our prayers, yet prayer cannot be relied on to produce instant results. We must pray, and pray, and pray . . . and still pray.

As Luke records, Jesus 'told them a parable to the effect that they ought always to pray and not lose heart.

Sometimes God does *not* answer our prayers; He makes us go on and on praying, because He has a very good reason for doing so: God is not uncaring, disinterested, off-duty, or even on strike. He sometimes allows prayer to go apparently unanswered in order to deepen our faith.

It reminds me of my efforts to learn to play the guitar. After the initial few hours, the fingers of a beginner's left hand become acutely sore, where they have been pressed on the strings, and the noise produced hardly seems worth the discomfort.

Yet, if the guitar is practised regularly daily, after a week or so, the skin over the tender finger-tips thickens, and the playing may even be beautiful. If playing is left off for a few months, the finger-tips then soften and the hardening process has to be begun again when the instrument is started again.

Praying may sometimes be like this. God wants us to mean business when we pray; as our prayer may go apparently unanswered, the finger-tips of our praying hands toughen with use; and our faith deepens and matures as we learn to trust God through a situation of apparent resistance to our request. If we decide to give it up because it doesn't work, our praying finger-tips soften again, and we find we have denied God a means of strengthening our faith. He allows this to happen at times to deepen our trust in Him, so that when life's storms hit us, we know that whatever happens He really *is* completely reliable.

Can our generation which is geared to constant activity and instant results be expected to 'wrestle' or 'persist' in prayer as the Christians of old did? Jesus makes no exception of us in His words about the need for prayer in the New Testament.

There are of course other reasons why God may

apparently not answer our prayers. Obviously if we are asking for the wrong things, we cannot expect God to answer as we hope He will; for instance, the girl praying for God to give her a visa to permit her to work in a certain country may be perplexed as to why, when God has apparently called her there, He does not move government officials to grant the prized visa. She may later discover the answer was simply that God wanted her to be willing to go and that, had she gone, she would have never met the man planned by God to be her husband.

God may apparently not answer prayer because it is not yet His time to do so; I may pray for the conversion of my friend, little realizing that God wants to delay this until the time when her husband, too, is willing to trust God and the couple can embark on their new Christian life together.

I sometimes have the nerve to dare to pray, and expect God to answer, when I know that I have frequently disobeyed Him. How can I expect an answer when I know I have lied, lost my temper, or indulged in petty pilfering? Were God to answer my prayer in the face of sin in my life, not yet put right with Him, it might then seem to me and to others that sin did not matter. As the Bible says, 'If I regard iniquity in my heart, the Lord will not hear me.'

However, I am sure that I cannot use any of the above as excuses for not now beginning to learn what it means to 'wrestle' and to 'persist' in prayer.

For me the big question relates to the fact that one day consists of only twenty-four hours. Where do we find the time in our Western culture for such time-consuming praying? I find that non-Christians challenge me; some of them have time to 'do their thing'; they make time for Buddhist or Hindu mystical meditation, Yoga and drug experimentation. Can we Christians say in all honesty that 'There isn't time'?

Perhaps I use, 'No time,' as an excuse, because I am afraid that if I really start to pray seriously then I would be labelled as a 'crank'. And, frankly, I am tempted sometimes to think of that missionary in India years ago, 'praying Hyde', as a crank, rather than as an example, when I read his biography. Perhaps he *was* a crank; but surely in God's eyes he was a very especially loved crank? He took God's word seriously, despite opposition from his fellow missionaries, who thought he was wasting time by praying so much instead of doing things. He went to an extreme: but he had a valid point, worthy of our consideration.

The Jesus of the New Testament seems to be looking for people who will hook-up to Him in prayer. Are we missing something precious that He longs to share with us?

9. CAUGHT UP IN SHARING

IT would be hopeless for me to try to remember how many times I have prayed myself, or heard others praying vaguely, 'If it is Your will, then please God will you . . .'

Yet, the Apostle John makes me wonder about this vague kind of praying by his clear-cut statement:
'This is why we have courage in God's presence; we are sure that He will hear us if we ask Him for anything that is according to His will. He hears us whenever we ask Him; since we know this is true, we know also that He gives us what we ask from Him.' (1 John 5, verses 14-15 TEV).

Jesus Himself definitely assures us, 'And I will do whatever you ask for in My name, so that the Father's glory will be shown through the Son. If you ask Me for anything in My name, I will do it.'

There is no happy haze or vagueness of escaping into 'If it be Thy will' about these words.

When I can accept these statements, I then find I have accepted something quite astounding. If I ask 'according to God's will' or 'in Jesus' name' then my requests will be granted.

Yet staggering limitations accompany these great

promises. How can I, an ordinary, not very spiritual Christian, ever presume that I know the will of the almighty, omnipotent God? I am tempted to feel that it is impossible and to accept defeat, before I've even begun to try. As I think about it, I know already that there *are* ways in which I can know God's will.

I can know God's 'general will' by reading His word. So I can presume, for instance, on the strength of the Bible words, 'The Lord is not slow to do what He has promised, as some think. Instead, He is patient with you, because He does not want anyone to be destroyed, but wants all to turn away from their sins.' (2 Peter 3, verse 9, TEV). So I can pray definitely for individual non-Christians to have a personal encounter with God. This is God's general will for the whole of mankind.

I don't have to pray, 'God, please help So-and-So to come face to face with You, *if it's your will.*' I know from the Bible that this *is* His general will for each individual man. I don't have to lecture myself about predestination and free will before *praying* for people.

Yet, experience does not prove it as simple as this sounds. When I pray for an individual, I may be conscious of a restraint in my prayers. I may be desperately concerned for one person, and yet not for another. One person may so occupy my consciousness that throughout the day I find that I am lifting him to God in prayer. There may be no rational explanation I can give for this. Why might it be so?

I remember one foggy day, while on leave in England, I was slogging through the family Monday morning wash, and clearing up the week-end's chaos in the house. As I sloshed wet clothes from washing-machine into spin-dryer (feeling more than somewhat bored, frustrated, and house-bound and not in the least 'spiritual'), I had a sudden urge to pray for a lady doctor in Thailand. This was such a unique experience to me, that I abandoned the wash, and went and squatted on the mat, in front of the sitting room fire.

'What is it, Lord?' I found myself praying, 'What's happened?'

There was no vision from Heaven. I had no clue what was going on.

The urge persisted, 'Pray for her; she needs your prayers.' So, I prayed for half an hour, in ignorance of why I was praying, and then sensing peace and freedom again, returned to clearing up the Monday morning debris. I said nothing to anyone about this; it wasn't the sort of thing that happened to people like *me*. However, I later learnt that, on that exact day, that doctor had been involved in a road accident in the hospital Land-Rover, along with a group of Thai Christians. No one had been badly injured; and the doctor, who had already had some eye trouble, had received a blow to her 'bad eye'. This at first seemed serious, but later settled, leaving her eyesight relatively unimpaired. Was this coincidence? I think not.

A similar incident happened recently to two medical students, who pray regularly for my husband and me. To them, we were an ideal married couple. They were surprised later to hear our story.

Missionary marriages may appear outwardly serene, but sometimes beneath the surface there is tension and strain. Due to pressure of work, my husband and I had begun to drift apart, although we still loved one another. We rarely saw one another to communicate, as we were both working full-time as doctors and off-duty hours rarely coincided. It was the thin end of the wedge. We could have existed like this indefinitely; but a close and precious relationship was in danger of disintegrating because of unthinking neglect. While I was away in Singapore for a month, my husband realized what was happening and came especially to meet me at the airport.

Much needed sorting out between us, and practical steps had to be taken to ensure that we had time together in the future, so that we did not drift into a similar situation again. After months of failure to communicate closely, it could have been hard for us suddenly to be frank and open with one another again; and we had only two days together before we were both back at the hospital on full-time duty. I do not think it was coincidence that, the very day when I arrived back and my husband and I began to sort things out seriously, these two medical students, who prayed regularly for us, felt that for no accountable reason they *must* stop everything and together pour out their hearts before God for us, believing us to be in some need. They later wrote to ask what had happened to us that day and were amazed at our reply. It was the last thing they would have imagined to happen to missionaries; but their missionaries are as human as they are.

I believe that these urges to pray come direct from

the Holy Spirit speaking to our hearts. If we believe the words of the Bible, we should be expecting this of Him, 'In the same way the Spirit also comes to help us, weak that we are. For we do not know how we ought to pray; the Spirit Himself pleads with God for us, in groans that words cannot express. And God, Who sees into the hearts of men, knows what the thought of the Spirit is; for the Spirit pleads with God on behalf of His people, and in accordance with His will.' (Romans 8, verses 26-27, TEV).

The Holy Spirit alone is the answer to how we ordinary Christians can possibly pray 'according to God's will' and in 'Jesus' name.' We cannot know this for ourselves, no matter how clever we are.

We can know God's general will as we read the Bible; but we are dependent on the Holy Spirit to make plain God's will in specific circumstances. He alone can enable us to pray specific prayers for specific circumstances.

Sometimes God's exact will may not have been revealed to us. Does that then mean we can't pray? I believe that we can still pray for a situation, although we are in the dark, and trust that the Holy Spirit will interpret our prayers to God.

It is almost as if we have to pray, 'Loving Heavenly Father, that situation is such a mess; humanly speaking I can't see how You can ever work it out; people are getting hurt and this hurts me; yet I come to You in trust that You will work and resolve all this.' I can then silently lift the people involved in loving concern to God and wordlessly entrust my weight of concern for the situation into His hands. God has no need for me to tell Him what I think His will ought to be in any situation, nor how my human reason things He might decide to work things out. The outcome may not be as anticipated, but God invited us to share in His solving of such situations, and to express our helpless dependence on Him by our prayers.

But how stupid can we get?

I have heard it said, 'God couldn't answer our prayers because we didn't tithe all our income.'

And from my own child, 'God won't answer *that* prayer of Daddy's, he forgot to say "For Jesus' sake".'

It is our privilege to learn to pray 'according to God's will' and in 'Jesus' Name.' But it is not to be expected that, because we do so, we will automatically and mechanically receive an answer, in response to the right actions and formulae. We cannot push a button to make God explode into action. Rather, we find that we are caught up in something beyond our normal selves; we are caught up in the amazing privilege of being allowed to share in God's work by our very feeble, and very human, prayers.

As the Holy Spirit interprets God's will to us, so I believe that we have a responsibility to seek God's guidance as to the people and situations for which He covets our prayers. Before beginning any project, many Christians seek guidance as to whether or not God wants them to undertake it or not.

Praying for others is sharing with God in His work in the world, and it may be a project God calls us to embark on with Him. We then need first to seek His guidance as to what sphere of working by praying He is calling us to share in. If God calls us to intercession, then it will make our praying more purposeful and meaningful. It becomes work to which we have been called by God.

Sharing such serious work with God is no laughing matter; it is no longer something we can shrug off as 'a bit of a waste of time', 'cranky' or 'old-fashioned'.

10. COFFEE AND INDIFFERENCE?

'THAT doesn't refer to me,' I reassure myself with a mental pat on the back as I listen to a record of Simon and Garfunkel. From the verandah of my Thai wooden house, I gaze over the rice fields. The maturing rice plants stretch to the horizon, covering the earth with a luxurious green carpet, slashed at intervals by the steel-blue streak of a kingfisher striking towards the water.

A Thai mother and children are combing the dykes between the paddy fields. I idly guess that they must be searching for edible crabs or frogs to sell as delicacies in the market. My surroundings are those of an idyllic, romantic, tropical country scene: no drought or floods this year.

The singing soothes me as I listen to it echoing across the fields towards the mother and her children,

'It's a still life water-colour of a now late afternoon,
As the sun shines through the curtain lace, and
    shadows wash the room,
And we sit and drink our coffee, couched in our
    indifference,
Like shells upon the shore; you can hear the ocean
    roar . . .
You read your Emily Dickenson and I my

Robert Frost,
We note our place with bookmarkers, and
measure what we've lost.
Like a poem poorly written we are verses out
of rhythm,
Couplets out of rhyme, in syncopated time . . .
Yes, we speak of things that matter, with words
that must be said,
An analysis worthwhile; is the theatre really
dead? . . .'

My mind wanders lazily as I listen to the music, and watch the family in the fields outside, *I'm* not indifferent . . . *I'm* a doctor working in a developing country, so none of this applies to me . . . *I'm* fully caring for those in need of help . . .

I absent-mindedly pick up a religious newspaper, and am surprised to read that a *man*, whom I respect through his writing, *wept* when he saw at first hand the plight of refugees from Bangladesh.

I turn to another edition of the same paper, and read the words of a sixth former, W. Johnston:

ME CARE, OF COURSE I CARE

Shake me from the golden slumber of escape
And drag me, naked, through the cobbled streets,
From now I am blind to all I see,
Or wish I were,
For what I see is so terrible
That involuntarily my eyes are blinded
By the gore, the death, the hunger,
That I pretend I cannot see,
As I sit in luxury, eating and sleeping

And spending in a day, a year of food,
A life of food, leaving a death,
But they are over there, and I am over here.
What can they be to me?
And yet I feel.
But that is all.
I make no effort.
I merely sit, and eat my toast and tea.

As I read, I gradually experience a deep sense of shame. While conscious of my contribution in a small way to relieving suffering, I discover that I am as yet unmoved by mass suffering in other parts of the world. If anything happened to the Thai family collecting crabs in the fields outside, I would rush out to help them without hesitating; but other people in other parts of the world fail to move me deeply.

Yet I can see with a somewhat shattering clarity, that there is absolutely no reason why I should be exempt from caring for people in other parts of the world, because I happen to be working in a country other than that of my birth. I expect my friends in England to care about Thailand; why should *I* then not care for other countries?

I may quote and agree in theory with John Donne's words, that no man is an island; and that the hurt of any one man is the hurt of myself. I may fleetingly respond to the poignant record published after Martin Luther King's death, asking, 'Who will care now that he is gone?', with a quick '*I'll* care.'

But when it comes to the point, I am forced to admit that I don't *do* anything. If I do get round to anything it is to practical action rather than praying. Might it be that, as with some of my friends. I too have been caught up in the swing of a pendulum. At one extreme of the swing, Christians might say 'Pray and everything will be all right', while at the other they say, 'Don't waste time praying, *do* something.'

For many of us action is the keynote; charity walks, giving time, energy and money to help. Perhaps we want to show the man in Sydney Carter's song that he is wrong when he sings, 'And God is up in Heaven but He doesn't do a thing; with a million angels watching, and they never move a wing.'

We want to show that God does care and love, and that nowadays He expresses His caring and love through us, His body here on earth. However, all this activity leaves next to no time or energy for intercessory prayer.

Somewhere in the middle of the swinging pendulum rests the balance of expressing concern both by prayer and by action.

As I write these words, the telephone rings, and I hear that one of my patients in the hospital is rapidly deteriorating, and looks as if he is dying. What do I do? Pray that he will come into communication with the living God before he dies; or run as fast as I can to the ward to see if any injections can save his life? The answer is simple. I run to the ward as fast as I can; but I pray all the way I'm running there. Prayer and action are not incompatible.

Those who are free both to pray and to act must establish a balance between the two. Of course some, who are house-bound, will make their valued contribution solely through prayer. But for young, energetic Christians, like myself, there should be time for *both* action and praying.

I find this all ties up with Paul's words, 'For the body itself is not made up of only one part, but of many parts . . . And so there is no division in the body, but all its different parts have the same concern for one another. If one part of the body suffers, all the other parts suffer with it; if one part is praised, all the other parts share its happiness.' (1 Corinthians 12, verses 12, 25, 26).

Years ago Calvin wrote, 'Our prayer must not be self-centred. It must arise not only because we feel our own need as a burden which we must lay upon God, but also because we are so bound up in love for our fellow-men that we feel their need as acutely as our own . . .. To make intercession for men is the most powerful and practical way in which we can express our love for them.

I now face a *double* challenge. I cannot exempt myself from caring for others in other parts of the world because I happen to be working and caring practically for ill people in Thailand. Concern and compassion for the whole world is as much my affair as it is of any other Christian in any part of the globe. My unity with my fellow-Christians throughout the world must find its expression both by my praying and by my practical action. The two are complementary; they do not compete with one another.

Love must express itself by seeking the highest good

for a loved one. Christian love involves action, and also praying. As Dr. H. E. Fosdick once said, intercessory prayer is 'love on its knees'.

All I can now do is come to God in deep humility, admitting 'Heavenly Father, I have failed You by my failure to care for others . . .' and dare to ask, 'God please make me care enough not only to act but to pray as well.'

11.   FOCUS ON INDIVIDUALS

Now that I am realizing the importance of intercessory prayer, I find the vastness of it all overwhelming.

John Wesley claimed, 'The world is my parish.' I wonder: is the whole world supposed to be my concern too? Am I to attempt to pray for everyone with their differing needs? Because if so, let's get it straight from the word 'go': the whole thing's too big. I am moved by mass suffering depicted on mass media. I am moved to pray vaguely for relief of suffering for whole groups of people in their huge unmet needs. Yet I still find that the practical key unlocking intercessory prayer for me is to focus my prayers on individuals, wherever possible.

Lack of knowledge of situations in certain countries may mean that I am unable to pray specifically: but for me this should be the exception rather than the rule.

Since intercessory prayer is work to which God calls me, I need to know clearly for whom I am to intercede. God guides in different ways. Guidance may come through an inexplicable inner urge. 'Pray for the victims of Hurricane . . .', 'Pray for that tribal group in . . .', 'Pray for so-and-so.'

Sometimes God guides by giving a definite responsibility to pray for some whom He has especially entrusted to our care: our families; those who have experienced Christ because we have introduced them to Him; close Christian and non-Christian friends; and those from our own churches in need of prayer for some particular reason.

God often draws us to pray for people with whom we already have a common bond, or with whom we share some common interest and concern. For instance, because I like dabbling in Christian communication by writing, I am concerned to pray for Christians, known to me by name only, who are seeking to communicate Christ through 'secular' channels and the mass media to non-Christians in England. Because I happen to be a missionary doctor, I am also concerned enough to pray for those known to me who are carrying out similar duties in other parts of the world.

God binds people together in prayer links which are deep, rich and rewarding. A childless couple, who once heard my husband and me speak for a few minutes on a platform, have taken us into their hearts as the children they never had. They pray for us like parents; our children's needs are like those of the grandchildren they long for. We know that they love us; although we have never been close personal friends we are united by their prayers.

A group of medical students once wrote to me saying, 'We've never really had our own missionary, so we want to take you on.' I gulped and wondered how to help them do this. I didn't know them and they didn't know me. They knew where Thailand was, but little else. Most of them knew even less about the missionary society with which I was serving. I wrote to them often, both as a group, and also as individuals; I dropped in on their meetings whenever I was in London, and gradually came to know them as people. Some of them grew to know me as a person who was human, like them. I shared my troubles; some reciprocated and shared theirs. I began to care about them as individuals. Some of them obviously cared about me. They shared deeply with us the dilemma we faced as missionary parents, at having to be separated from our children. They become involved with us in this. Over several years they put about £600 into a trust fund, to be saved up to fly our children out to visit us, when they had to return to school in England, and we were working in Thailand. When we were short-staffed, two of them offered to come and work as housemen in our hospital if it would help.

I knew I could rely on their constant prayer-support, and that in times of crisis they were behind us, solid as rock. Their prayers are my secret treasure-hoard of inestimable value. The students' interest initially started from a conviction that they ought to do something about missionaries. Because they were medical students, they chose a missionary doctor in whom to take an interest; and God joined the pray-ers and those prayed for in a very special family-like bond. We knew in Thailand by first airmail as soon as an engagement was announced, or exams were passed, and the tape of a wedding was dispatched airmail for us to share in the joy of the bridal couple immediately. In a very precious way we were joined to one another. I found too, that I cared for them, and it was easy for me to reciprocate and intercede for them, as individuals, when they wrote sharing their problems.

This group showed me how deeply Christians, starting from scratch, can become involved with one another in a bond of intercession. From the first we met on an equal footing; we acknowledged that we all had faults and failings; that the missionary full-time Christian worker was no better or holier than the Christian in the secular employment to which God has called him. The group also began to understand what it must be like for me, being me, to be in my situation. They knew my temperament, and how I reacted. They could stand in my shoes, and experience empathy in the different situations in which I found myself. Some of them could clearly project themselves into my situation and pray with deep knowledge. They did their homework. Some of them collected maps, books, and magazines, to find out all they could about Thailand and the O.M.F. They shared their findings with the others.

Interest waxed and waned through their student careers, but there was always a nucleus, who stuck to praying for us, because they felt so bound up with us that they could not drop us. Now they have qualified, and scattered, and I shall miss them deeply.

I believe that the principles lying behind their prayers for us, are applicable to many situations for which God may call us to prayer.

I have had the rich gift given to me, as a missionary,

of seeing and experiencing the intercessory prayer of others, as 'love on its knees', love lavished—for no human reason—on me.

It is humbling and exhilarating to be at the receiving end of such a gift.

12. IMAGINATION AND INVOLVEMENT

I DON'T think I'll ever dare say them again: those glib, pious words of farewell with which I've often reassured a friend, or a person in need, 'I'll be praying for you,' when all I really meant was 'May God bless and strengthen you.'

I now know that to promise to pray, and then to break such a promise, is no light matter.

In future, when I give the assurance, 'I'll be praying for you,' it will only be said when there is a firm intention, with the help of God, to undertake to intercede for that person.

Despite the fact that I am a missionary myself, I still do not necessarily find it easy to pray for other missionaries. I have the advantage of being given certain insights not given to the non-missionary; but this is not always enough. I come from a church which has sent many missionaries into many different parts of the world. I happen to be one of their representatives in Thailand; yet I am still a member of my church in England; and so the other missionaries are still *my* representatives, in other parts of the world. (The fact that I happen to live abroad does not negate this.)

I sometimes find it hard to pray for these other

missionaries. I have to ask myself, 'What are their lives like? What must it be like to be a nurse, having to run a mission hospital alone, with no doctor? What must it be like to be the first Anglican deaconess to be ordained into the Church of England ministry in Hong Kong? What must it be like to work amongst a poverty-stricken Indian community in South America? What must it be like to be a radio programmer with the Far East Broadcasting Association in the Seychelles? What must it be like to be preparing literature aimed at Moslems?'

These are just a few of the ways in which *my* representatives, from my church, are seeking to share Christ in other parts of the world. I have a responsibility to pray for them.

There are some basic ways in which I can help myself go about this job of fulfilling my special responsibility to pray for these missionaries. I can find out all that I can about their country and about the missionary society with which they are working. I can get the magazines and newsletters issued by their society, and borrow any tapes and slides that may be available. Then I can ask to receive (and contribute towards the cost of distributing) the individual missionary's regular circular letters.

This list may involve considerable exercise of the imagination, if the missionary concerned tends to write rather boring letters. He often can't help himself if he writes dully, and in clichés. I know that he may be blissfully unaware of this fact, and I have to make allowances for him. But, should the occasion ever arise, I might drop a tactful hint that there are Christian writing courses available that would help make his letters more interesting. I have to learn to ignore the clichés, the Victorian language; I have to work to make a dull letter come alive through my imagination.

For instance, a single girl may drop the remark in a letter, 'It's sometimes lonely here, being so far from the town.' Were she more poetic and less inhibited, she might express herself as this single missionary shared with me,

> 'No lover makes my kiss his daily quest.
> No hand across the table reaches mine.
> No precious baby nestles at my breast.
> No-one to need my love. Where is the sign
> That God, my Father, loves me? Surely He
> Creates this wealth of love to overflow.
> How can it be that no-one who wanted me
> Has become mine? Why did I tell them "no"?
> But do they really matter, all the "why's"?
> Could all the answers take away the pain,
> Or all the reasons really dry my eyes,
> Though from Heaven's courts? No, I would
> weep again.
> My God, You have saved me from Hell's black
> abyss;
> Oh, save me from the tyranny of bitterness!'

A somewhat sermonic letter from a missionary working in a war area, might contain a phrase like, 'Our times here may be getting short, as the enemy seems to be getting nearer.' Not much in that, but imagination can make this remark spring to life.

Another missionary friend, working in Laos, explains more eloquently:

' ''That was the most miserable month I've ever spent in Laos!'' I said, as I tore a page off the calendar in 1968.

'Most of the month we had slept in our clothes in a village away from home, because of the risk of bombing of our home at night.

'We were allowed home by day only, but not to sleep there. Our neighbours slept out in the woods. Christian friends advised us to move to the big city. We tried to visualize every possibility. Since our house was near a target area for incoming mortar bombs, a miss on the target could be a direct hit on us.

'By day we were prepared to jump on to a plane at a moment's notice. It was hard to discern the Lord's voice amid frenzied rumours all around us. There is such a fine margin between alertness and plain worry.

'Although we would rather live by the Bible words, ''I will trust and not be afraid'', we found more realistic words to be, ''When I am afraid I will trust Thee.''

'Eventually it seemed that the Lord's promise was summed up in the words from Psalm 91, verse 10, ''No evil shall befall you, no scourge come near thy tent. For He will give His angels charge of you to guard you in all your ways.''

'I didn't know how near ''near'' might be; but God's promise was enough. We were able to ignore the quivers of the house, and the rumblings of the bombs.

'Why stay in such a place? We could not escape the sense of God's call. The thoughts of moving elsewhere gave no peace. In fact there were no Divine marching orders yet. God wanted us here; ready and available to those who needed us.

'So we continue on, not nobly or bravely, as some unrealistic and romantic friends imagine, but acutely aware of our own weakness and vulnerability. In this precarious spot we continue to revel in the Meadow Lark's song in the garden, but remain on edge; constantly on call for emergency evacuation. We continue to enjoy the exquisite tropical sunsets; but dread the following unknowns of the noisy nights in the jungle village. We live always on the edge of strain.'

I can help myself to intercede for others, if I can learn to read between the lines in the letters from those who are not very good at expressing themselves on paper. It then comes as little surprise when the young, attractive, very new missionary for whom I have been praying, writes to say that she is getting married; I have already read between the lines of her circular letters and seen that she needs a husband; and her marriage is the answer to my prayers. Nor am I surprised when another missionary friend writes to say that her engagement is 'off'. I know her well enough to have read between the lines of what she *didn't* say in the letter announcing her engagement. I could see that she was facing the recurring crisis of the single lady missionary: that of the shortage of eligible single males. She was getting engaged to the only man around, regardless of whether he was suitable or not, because he was her only hope; I knew and felt deeply for her in this. But her letter saying that the engagement was broken, was an answer to my prayers that God would lovingly show her without her getting too hurt in the process.

Missionaries are not always given the gift of frankness. They may have many reasons for not sharing their real problems with their prayer partners. Some may, by nature, be reticent people, who would never share anything deep with anyone. Some may feel that so much is expected of them that they dare not let down those who support them. They thus, unthinkingly, and not intending hypocrisy, tend to dwell on their successes rather than their failures.

To me, the key to this lies in a willingness to expose oneself to others. A prayer partner of mine might write to me, 'My three children nearly drove me up the wall today, so I felt especially close to you with yours, and coping with them in the heat of the tropics; it made me pray especially for you and the children.' Or a doctor writes, 'I made such a mistake about one of my patients today that I could kick myself . . . it made me pray especially for wisdom for you in treating your patients . . .' These pray-ers have expressed themselves as fallible, and by some quirk of human nature, I am quick to respond to such, by sharing my real needs with them.

The person who writes, 'I praise God for you and your wonderful work', gives me a temporary glow of self-satisfaction; because like everyone else I appreciate being appreciated. However, the glow wears off rapidly, because I know that the writer of those letters has no idea how hard it is to keep going through the Thai hot season when I'm dead beat and the hospital is at its busiest; nor how overwhelmingly discouraging it can be to see people meeting Christ in the hospital, then losing touch with Him again when they leave the hospital, because there is no-one to follow them up in their village in the back-of-beyond. To such a writer I would tend to concentrate on those finding Christ, and to make little mention of the lack of follow-up.

Similarly, the one who writes in the vein, 'You must be wonderfully spiritual sending your children away to school so young. My faith isn't strong enough. I admire you tremendously', leads me to want to write despairingly, 'Can't you understand, I'm ripped to shreds every time I put the children on the train . . . the agony of separation hurts too deeply to be described . . . but what can I do . . . if my husband and I go, who will bring Christ to this area? . . . please don't admire me! There's nothing to admire. I'm human, hurt, and need your help.' But such a letter does not (in my experience) get the desired response. The writer has decided that he is going to admire the missionary; and admire him he will!

If I can imagine what it must be like to be the one for whom I am praying, then I find that I can begin to intercede for that person. My imagination leads me on to want to be more deeply involved with him in his own life. This involvement leads to caring;

caring to love; and love to intercession.

I may never meet the one for whom I pray; but I may come to love him enough to offer him one of the most precious gifts one person can offer another; that of intercession, 'love on its knees'.

The choice is mine.

God will never force me into this. He longs for my co-operation and sharing of His work by my prayers. God's invitations have already been issued.

I can respond with a whole-hearted, 'Yes, God . . . I'll go all the way with You in praying for that person . . .'

Or I can mumble an evasive, 'Not right now . . . . perhaps tomorrow . . .': which might as well have been said as 'No!' in the first place.

Or I can have a half-hearted dabble, to make me feel good, and give up when I've had enough.

It took the death of a friend to make me wake up to the importance of praying for other people. I now know part of the theory. Will her death bear fruit in my practising what I have learnt?

The choice is ours.

What answer will we give God?